Good Hair, Bad Hair
By Kristen Telley

About The Author

Kristen Telley was born July 9. 1994 in Greenville, South Carolina. Although a South Carolina native, the author was raised mostly in Alabama. Kristen graduated from Judson College, a women's Baptist college located in the historic Civil Rights community of Marion, Alabama.

As a Judson student, Kristen was able to participate in several civil rights service and learning opportunities. Amongst those opportunities one of the greatest was the ability to work closely with Civil Rights activists, playwright, actress, and poet, Dr. Billie Jean Young. This opportunity also opened doors for the author to work with and meet several civil rights figures and important black leaders, such as Albert Turner Jr., Congressman John Lewis, Joanne Bland, Della Maynor, Congresswoman Terri Sewell, and many more.

Kristen graduated with a degree in psychology and criminal justice. The author's greatest passion is to educate, uplift, and encourage the black community, especially black youth. Good Hair, Bad Hair was written to encourage black children to accept, embrace, and love their hair texture exactly the way it is. The author's goal is also to teach black children not to categorize themselves or others with labels such as good hair or bad hair because all blackness is beautiful.

About The Illustrator

Marguerite C. Wright brings words to life through her artwork. She has loved art since childhood. She has created illustrations for several children's books.

Marguerite is an digital and traditional illustrator and portrait artist. She is originally from Detroit, Michigan. She received a Bachelor's degree from Western Michigan University in Graphic Design. She taught Graphic Design at Westwood College in Chicago area.

Marguerite is thankful for the opportunity to do the illustrations for the book Good Hair, Bad Hair.

She recieved Honorable mention for her digital watercolor painting at the MDAC 2021 Exhibition, in the Bay area of California and virtual exhibit!

She presently lives in a Chicago south suburb with with her husband and sons.

You can visit her website at: **www.margueritesart.com**

What is good hair? What is bad hair?

This is Destiny. Her hair is short, curly, and bouncy. Does she have good hair, or does she have bad hair?

This is Imani. Her hair is short too, but kinky and puffy. Does she have good hair, or does she have bad hair?

This is Khalil. He has spunky dreadlocks. Does he have good hair, or does he have bad hair?

Khalil

This is Jaidon. His hair is tall. His hair is curly too! Does he have good hair, or does he have bad hair?

Saidon

This is Logan. His hair is faded like Jaidon's, only his is shorter and kinky. Does Logan have good hair, or does he have bad hair?

Logan

What about you? Would you say that you have good hair, or would you say you have bad hair? Is your hair kinky, or is your hair curly? Or do you have spunky locs, like Khalil?

Let's think and talk about why we call hair good or why we call hair bad.

What do you think makes hair good?

What do you think makes hair bad?

Some people think that coarse or kinky hair, like Imani's hair or Logan's hair, is bad, while coily or bouncy hair, like Destiny's hair or Jaidon's hair, is good.

Black people's hair is a lot like flowers. It needs water and other nutrients to grow and to flow! When you water flowers, the roots in the soil drink up the water. The water then flows up into the flowers' stems and leaves. This helps them grow. Water also moves nutrients (like vitamins) from the soil into the flowers. Our hair and our bodies work the same way; they need water and nutrients. Our hair gets the nutrients it needs when we water it and eat plenty of fruits, vegetables, and healthy foods. These nutrients are even good for our skin. Don't forget, you also have to drink plenty of water, too!

Oil your scalp! This is also a very important way for our hair to get its nutrients by locking in the moisture.

Moisture makes our curls come alive. When we put products like creams, oils, and butters on our hair, they help keep our hair moist and make our curls pop and shine! Remember, everyone's hair is different, so we may not use the same things to make our hair look healthy that someone else uses.

Many people use spray bottles to water their hair just like they use them to water plants too.

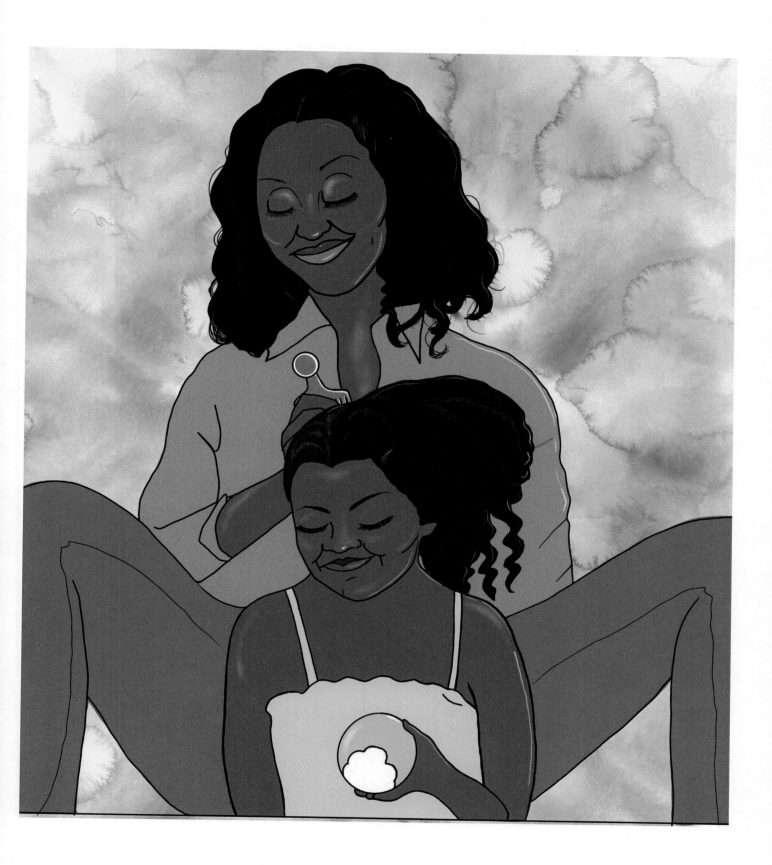

Some of us have hair like orange daylilies. These are beautiful flowers that don't need as much water as some flowers to grow.

Some of us have hair a lot like gorgeous swamp sunflowers. These happy flowers need plenty of water; more water than daylilies need. Does this mean that swamp sunflowers aren't pretty too? No way! It only means swamp sunflowers need something different in order to grow too.

Kinky, or very curly, hair is like swamp sunflowers, it needs more water. Kinky hair is mostly naturally dry, so it needs plenty of water! Although some of us have bouncy curls like Destiny, or coily hair like Jaidon, it still needs water to survive; just like flowers.

Just like there are different types of flowers, there are different types of hair. Just like flowers, every hair type is beautiful in its own way.

Like flowers, growth takes time. Be patient. Wait. Water your hair and wait for the bloom!

So, what is good hair? What is bad hair? The answer: there is no such a thing! Your hair, all black people's hair, is beautiful in its own way. Whether it is curly and bouncy. Whether it is kinky and puffy. Whether you have spunky locs. Whether it is tall and faded. Whether it is short and coily. Whether it takes a little water, or a lot. Whether it takes a long time to grow and to flow, it is okay because eventually, it will bloom!

Dedicated to Dr. Billie Jean Young

This book is dedicated to Dr. Billie Jean Young. Dr. Young was a marvelous teacher and mentor especially to black youth. As a former student and spiritual daughter, I made a vow to pass the torch by educating, uplifting, and empowering the black community and black youth. Dr. Billie Jean Young strongly encouraged education, love, and pride of black history and culture. This book is also dedicated in her honor because she taught me to accept and love my kinky hair. For so long what I thought was nappy and dreadful became my crown and glory.

The very first time Dr Young saw my natural hair, she cried. Her eyes gleamed with admiration. The day her teary eyes pranced around the kinky puff that crowned my head I became proud of my hair.

Rest In Heaven my dear spiritual mother.

Made in United States
Orlando, FL
28 August 2024